Battery Rocks

With this powerful new collection Katrina Naomi becomes one of the foremost poetic voices of her generation. Profoundly connected to the natural world and distinguished by an informed ethical stance regarding our historic moment, her poems combine colloquial and formal energies in their linguistic reach. Vulnerability and feistiness, love, grief, tenderness, are grounded here in experience, and engage with the reader at every level. Immersion of being is here, either in the sea off Penzance where this poet regularly swims, or in the ocean of human concerns which this poet presents with living vital necessity. This is a collection of accomplished register, of relish for life, shot through with awareness of human vulnerability; a poet who plumbs the depths, be those of love, of the ocean, of fear, and challenge; a poet who speaks from the discipline of the heart, in poems wrought with craft and insight. An essential collection.

– Penelope Shuttle, author of *Lyonesse*

Katrina Naomi's Battery Rocks is a book of nature specifically about the sea. Naomi's nature is one that troubles the relationship of people to nature. Instead of nature being a proxy for the spiritual order of the world Naomi examines the effect of nature on one's physical and emotional life. Naomi creates and examines a deeper more vulnerable personal relationship with nature. Each poem rolls in and out like the sea and refreshes like a wild swim. Highly enjoyable. Get it now.

– Roger Robinson, author of *A Portable Paradise*

In these salt-soaked, wind-swept poems, Katrina Naomi explores wild swimming as an act of resistance, of persistence, as a type of prayer. These surprising poems weave together to create a beautiful love letter that encompasses the sea and the creatures that live in it, the changing seasons, and finally the human body and the miraculous things it is capable of.

– Kim Moore, author of *All the Men I Never Married*

Katrina Naomi finds fascinating ways to reboot the life away from the hurly burly and yet to remain fiercely invigorated, to be at one in the elemental, to ask the big questions about place and what it means to be at home. She achieves this with compassion, kindness and humour in a sequence that enriches and expands its insights as it is read.

– Daljit Nagra, author of *Indiom*

Battery Rocks

Katrina Naomi

Seren is the book imprint of
Poetry Wales Press Ltd.
Suite 6, 4 Derwen Road, Bridgend,
Wales, CF31 1LH

www.serenbooks.com
Follow us on social media @SerenBooks

ISBN: 978-1-78172-754-6
ebook: 978-1-78172-760-7

A CIP record for this title is available from the British Library.

The publisher acknowledges the financial assistance of the Books Council of Wales.

Cover artwork: Nina Leen, Au Bord De La Terre.

Printed in Bembo by 4Edge Limited, Essex.

for all who depend on the sea

Contents

"Whatever will you do down there?" they asked.

— Iris Murdoch, The Sea, The Sea

and what I heard was my whole self
saying and singing what it knew: *I can.*

— Denise Levertov, 'Variations on a Theme by Rilke', *Breathing the Water*

AUTUMN

Fickle Lover

Ours is not a relationship of equals.
You're passionate, rough, violent. So much
is an act – you're always on display – I want you
all to myself. Of course, you're unfaithful, you swim
with anyone, moshing their thighs, their breasts,
knocking them out with your rush.

At one time, I could choose
whether to be in love with you. I do my best
to ignore your conquests. Instead, I think
of when you're away, how you leave me
gifts – razor shells, man o' war, jags of glass –
fragile reminders of your own tough love.

I need your chill; can't help myself.
You swoosh round my brain, frolicking
with neurones, make my skin fit me, tighter,
tighter, after I've plunged right in. I'm going
deeper. I can't consider what you want –
pinning me, scraping my limbs along rocks.

I've learnt to say no.
Despite your allure, I won't go to you at night.
But sunrise, I'll be waiting for you, having
shifted my day around your tides;
my primitivism seduced – loving
how you run, spuming, towards me.

Golden Shovel: After Iris Murdoch

The sea is something that happens to you. An mor. An mor. This
is what I've learned as I rush each morning
like a penitent – diarghen – before a decent shrine. I
cannot – ha ny vynnav vy – help myself. I know this is simply
stated – forgive me – words mean so little since I dived
head and heart into
high tide, every pore, every follicle, alert. It goes deep
this affair. They say I was dunked in the water
at three days old. I've never dried myself off
never wanted terra firma – the
sensible, the understood. That isn't living. The sea rocks
me awake, like sex; good sex, is the nearest
to swimming on a chill, bright day, out to
the far west – further. An mor. You'll say I'm bragging but this is the
place to swim – to be freed, away from the house
– its reminders of being settled, where
you find all the oughts and shoulds, those horrid visitors. They
– their commanding voices – can't be heard as I descend
into lanow, its bleak welcome, its byrla, one I almost
understand, am warmed by, despite its sheer
fall into nothingness out past the rocks. Yet
this neuvya – this swimming – still terrifies with
the light unable to filter through the folds
of cold, into the deep of under, how it blends, forms, reforms. And
darkness gathers like a shoal; where ledges
of granite glitter-shout. They are enough
to stop me sirening up, to
the known – aswonnys. Who wouldn't make
every effort to stay? Yes, this is an obsession, a
glorious reacquaintance – kales – precarious
at best. I plunge from the rough-cut stairway

*Kernewek (Cornish) words: an mor – the sea; diarghen – penitent or barefoot;
ha ny vynnav vy – and I don't want to; lanow – a rising tide; byrla – embrace;
neuvya – to swim; aswonnys – known; kales – difficult.*

One-Sided Conversation with a Hydrozoan

Pink mini monster, exaggerated bubble
of gum
        blown from the Indian Ocean
against October drifts of black-green weed

your gassy bag of sail crimped like a pasty
You've swum a colossal distance
        to lie on a Sunday beach
Portuguese, at least by name, war-like

They say you're no jellyfish. I offer a guarded welcome
It's your tropical tentacles –
        the blue of Curaçao cocktails –
that do the damage, stunning

fish, wiping welts along swimmers' bodies
Your lacy, lengthy, bike chains
        your party poppers of venom
mingle with themselves, stinging bladder wrack to oblivion

You've a freedom a person can admire, your own food
and transport, your ease in reproduction
        a kitschy colour scheme
to die for, or at least sense keenly. Let's say you leave your mark

I respect your beauty, your gaiety
But
    dear
        silent
            killer
why this display, why all the flashy warning? You're a sun king
a samurai in his finery, an Uma Thurman on Marazion sands

I'm unsure how many choices a hydrozoan gets to make

I could choose to end your life. Instinct says
bury you – you may do me harm

        But I want you
              gorgeously alive

15

Environmental Poem No 5784

There are rules
　　　in deep water

Standing's
　　　for that abandoned thing

　　　　　Land

The Sea & Me

She throws herself at me, as I cling
to the lull of mossed rocks, washes me

away into her shouty body, jumps up like a geyser;
jagged hills rush my head, she plays, allows little time for me

to find my breath, snort a mouthful, before her grey mountain looms
I yell into the bay for the hell of it, this tumble

of fear and exhilaration; the mountains kill
themselves, breaking their iced lava on the rocks at the unloved edge

of town. Could this be my last swim? No one has more stake here
than the sea. Ours is a pact of sorts, both of us revelling

in our own fashion; she sends a cordillera, an advancing range of snowy peaks,
I could dive, coward-like but kick my heels, thrust

wrists summitwards, my air bursts the wave with a whoop
of survival; the sea grins: *till tomorrow*

The Days of Not Swimming

The extremities are easy. Only / the middle is a puzzle
– Louise Glück – 'Heaven and Earth'

those middling days, without risk
without the sea

choosing whether I'll drip up the rough-
cut steps or be pinioned bone against rock

days when a hot shower is all
rose and geranium soap
no sand, grit or *Chondrus crispus* in the bath

no need to turn the dial
further and further to the red
for my chest to feel that welcome

burn; followed by a morning
when I munch my marmite toast
it's almost the end of *Today*

> as opposed to shovelling in toast and beans
> or mushrooms or tofu, or all three, like coal to an engine

> on its first run uphill; when I don't
> wedge a scalding water bottle
> in the waistband of my jeans til mid-afternoon

> those fair days
> when I don't walk with a sailor's sway

> when a heart beats steady, my nose doesn't
> flood, when I've topics of conversation beyond

> high tide; days when I dress with conviction
> after spending an extra 45 minutes
> under the duvet, warm

> and slightly dead

18

Thoughts Over Hot Chocolate

it is cold
        my costume's thinner than my childhood red and blue one-piece
my toes no longer reach the sea floor
        beneath them so many glistening mouths
i have seen the size of those mouths
        some say we were once all fish
beyond the land a sense of belonging
        i vogue in blue and green and grey
from further out from a new angle i look at my town
        i cannot be reached
i am a girl again
        sea blondes my hair
a wave propels me a wave which could never be a friend
        i am sucked back by this wave
no longer having to stand like everyone else
        i understand ships better
emails have not been invented
        the drag of salt on my skin its itch and tighten its delicious frost
i have always swum
        my heart bangs in understated gratefulness
danger is a mild attraction one i wish to honour
        in the sea i am alone
mackerels' retro patterning appeals
        i'm a different animal now far from mannered
it is cold
        it is no longer cold

Swimmers' Brag

My dripping limbs I faintly stretch,
And think I've done a feat today
– George Gordon Byron – 'Swimming from Sestos to Abydos'

Hail's white peas hit the bedroom window, as if to split themselves, or the
glass
Perhaps it'll blow over?
      Nah, let's do it

We dash for the harbour, swim from quay to quay
    Boats loom through murk; it lacks the thrill of swimming off the
rocks
         Hail shifts to mizzle

Patting myself dry on the slipway, I raise my cormorant elbows, pull a loud
dress over my head
     The cossie sits at my ankles like a dejected dog

A woman approaches, she only swims Thursdays
       It was just too bumpy at the Battery

We're all apologetic when we can't swim in the open sea; the harbour's a
poor second
      Yeah, I know, it's too rough, no point

Though when me and Tim were on our way down, John, in his 70s, was
already back up the hill, hair slick from his swim
     He called across the road to us
   A bit of hard work on the way out and you're pushed back on the return,
it's great

John marking his territory, making it known he'd taken the risk off the
rocks; that he's braver than us
     He'd have spluttered on every stroke

A gentle brag, then

I tell the woman who only swims Thursdays, the water's warm
        She hesitates
                No, really

I wring out my navy one-piece, carry it by the drippy straps, back up the
hill, through town, so everyone can see
                Towel round my neck like a trophy

So Good

she said dripping salt water
on the cement of land each pore
a little volcano of happy
each hair reaching out to sun
in that loved-up way of arm hair
while feet stand
damp under the solemn robe
cold but mostly oblivious
now they're doing their ordinary
flat thing after the flex & push at fluidity

face has its shades on
smiling morningwards
face likes this heightened polarised
view of the Lizard's sliver
feet are indifferent preferring
the sight of fluffy fibres
on the inside of striped navy socks
face is pleased possibly ecstatic
& brain is taking
a moment

having kept her alive
powering her out to second buoy
& back reminded her when it's safe
to breathe in & when to spit out

brain's also pleased
she wasn't vain enough to try
to swim further
that she understands her body
temperature's dropping that it was time
to push off

from the aqua blue-
tiled wall of underwater imagination
to kick towards the tiny church of town
against tide & ego
to the rust-grip of railing
haul up to the rock & steps

brain has remembered hot chocolate
in her bag but hasn't yet impressed
upon her the urge to drink
most days her ears listen
for her body's cooling
face is still upturned bathing in light
ears attuned to the roar on rocks
beneath still-brown feet
brain gets her reluctant attention
cocoa has her heart spiral
as it does when she's scared of the waves'
surge or that she'll swim too far one morning

for now heart's glad to be bopping
in one place in love with veins & arteries
flushing its love all over her trying
to talk with brain even if brain's a bully
can brain encourage her
to zip up her fleece?
not even brain has that much sway –
she's still in lull to the language of sea-shush
sound of sun on tide
still believes in summer

i.m. of Sarah Everard

After a shaky week

    I shiver back in

News of another woman

    I swim mechanically

shoving the sea away

Memories surface

    of my own attack

36 years ago

He still swims alongside

    clambers on my legs, my head, my back

With each stroke I strike the water

    thankful for my strength that night

I've learned to swim in rough seas

Tattoo

for Kim Moore

No one can touch me
I swim alone to the third buoy

An inked cloud absorbs the light, the ocean loses its blue
Swimming back, a pulse of tide lifts me to the rocks' steps

Biceps straining, I heave up and out; the water drains my weight
A new awareness of this body in tight, navy one-piece

No one else here; I hold a flamenco-print towel to my face
wriggle out of the costume

To my left a man, on the rocks, flexing swallows on each arm; he
turns, mid-puff on a thin roll-up; looks along the length of me

I force jogging bottoms up over wet thighs, cram a T-shirt down; everything sticks
sprint barefoot for the road, to cars, people, a yellow-white Council truck

I've met those swallows before

The Sea Speaks

I sense her fear;
    she wants me
to lie down with her
    I won't be commanded
could call off my waves
    go flat flat
& she'll swim out
    of her range
to her goal of the fourth buoy
    (I know these things
she invests so much
    time with me)
then I'll summon the waves back
    have them fierce
experience her splutter-panic
    how she'll struggle not to cry
I know how much of me
    she'll breathe in
how much her lungs
    will take as I hit her
full in the face
    perhaps only every third
or fourth wave
    I can be generous like this
Tomorrow, she'll be back
    telling herself she's getting braver
that at 56 (or 57)
    she's fitter than she's ever been
You see why she returns to me
    Maybe you'd care
to join her, slip off the rocks
    She won't mind
a little promiscuity
    She says otherwise but I *really* know her
better than she knows herself
    Come on; dive in
I'll go gentle with you

Golden Shovel: After Monique Roffey's
The Mermaid of Black Conch

I go early to the rocks, my heart
full of bombs; that feeling
trying to shove war away but Palestine's in
my every thought. The sea churns. I pull my
clothes off. The wind rushes this coward chest
nipples like spent bullets. My lover's away. I would
swim further but lack verve. I come
alongside the first buoy, a warning to
shipping; a bobbing place of almost protection; the
realisation of luck in this life; sea
as companion with
its tiny dangers; these I court. There was the old me
the human rights worker, I
managed 13 years; found I couldn't feel
anymore. I'll confess it
became too much. Even
here, I rarely dive deep; I protect myself. Now
I see the imaginary borders; how long
I can swim for. Others aren't so fortunate. Time
was, I did things differently. It's so much later

Asterias Rubens

It's only as I clamber out, onto the rocks, my sparky breath white
in the morning air, that I see her – pymphys – five legs. They say she's common.

She looks anything but, lazing in a crevice in the cold, clear, nudging water,
creamy yellow, like an inside-out banana skin but larger; her limbs elongated,

as if she were an ice cream cornet, squidgy, vulnerable. I could've stepped on her.
She's as indifferent to me, of course, as the cormorant throwing the curve of his neck

to the deep, as the turnstones – their Aztec wing pattern – are truly indifferent, as their
wingspans skim the reach of my breaststroke. I'm just another land animal; one who fails

to thrive underwater – unlike the starfish – relaxing in her own salty galaxy,
each inhale as easy and unhurried as the next, breathing through her trail of feet.

Kernewek (Cornish) word: pymphys – starfish (literally five digits)

28

Cutting Through

A huge calm this morning, mist, waves stilled.
The shock of cold water, an immersion
more powerful after a night of burning Mum's diaries –

not knowing if I could. Her presence scrawled the room
with smoke; then came the fire alarm's shriek.
I opened the door three times before it would silence.

Here, the unnatural quiet of the bay, after her words
writhed in the stove. Triggered by more than smoke,
I hadn't expected tears. I burnt what I hadn't read,

traced the drugged hand of her last four nights –
her giant orange felt-tip scribble heady as whisky.
She found a wild voice in her final hours, cutting through

the peace of the bay. I felt my hand move to the door.
On the path, a version of her. Recognisable.
I'm used to speaking to her; chose my words:

Mum, please believe mine was an act of love;
I wanted you free of the page, free of your diaries;
needed to let you go.

With each stroke, I tell myself, she understands.
Mist gathers on the horizon;
smoke from a known – much-missed – fire.

On Distance

I always start with the sky
said the artist
with what's furthest away

≈ 1 ≈

The sun is something
to sense rather than study

The horizon somewhere I walk to
on those long stretches
across moors or desert

I can't walk to the sky
with no ladder or sequoia to carry me

My climbing skills undeveloped
just the squat
apple tree of my childhood was enough
to sense myself closer to the sun

I climbed to a flat roof
where I couldn't be found
Further away from Mum & my sister
but still close to them

I loved them

My father was further away
doing something similar
couldn't be found   was rarely on the ward
rarely at the hospital when he said he was

Did Mum know?   She watched him
drive off in the pale blue Morris Minor

≈ 2 ≈

A balloon's overhead some days   serene
but its noise disturbs with a vicious heat
The balloon is little more than a wicker box
a distant picnic basket   without a lid

would do nothing to save you
crashing into a field   I've never pictured my father
falling   though he fell
in an orchard   is buried alongside his dogs
(I never knew he liked dogs)

Today the sky is free of balloons
the sun is probably up there
but what's furthest away is debatable

≈ 3 ≈

Other times what's furthest away is the yellow buoy
Invitation to a swimmer   command to boats
I once swam to the buoy   to the dark blue edge
of the shipping lane   the start of very deep water
the ledges beneath like rows of shelves

Today the buoy feels too far
Courage is furthest from me

Courage is not a flashy colour such as lime   violet
or tangerine
Courage is a glossy brown

I haven't the strength   It's too far   You shouldn't attempt such a swim alone
My inner voice part-soothes   part-frustrates

Clouded with Caution   I'm a duller brown
the shade of school uniforms   the colour
I've known since convent

Those clothes have shrunk
Without you   I can't locate the skirt's eye
& hook   unknot the stripey tie

The elastic of the Panama hat has grown
into my neck   a strand of wire fence
folded into the bark of an oak   almost welcome

I can't free the elastic   my jaw can't lengthen
if not a swan's neck   an imitation of one

But with you alongside
the dull brown fades to the tan on my skin
The mis-shaped straw hat has COURAGE printed on its band

I swim out to the buoy   the shipping lane
my arms glossy as the flank of a horse
who's happy to stand in the shade   rippling the muscles
of her back   avoiding the everyday irritations
saving her energy
for what's important to a horse
keeping herself to herself in the shade of an oak

                ≈ 4 ≈

What's in the wicker basket or the violent noise of the mind?
For months after Mum died
I'd be pushed back into the pillow
long fingers shoving me
the big hand stopping me from going to the window
to look for the yellow-orange light

Now there's this sweet giggle of news
something I'm learning to carry for when I need it

An extra kick in my legs   all the way to the buoy
Because I've said yes to a gathering of poets

Momentarily   famous poets' names are aligned with my own
I remind myself they were ordinary too   but died young
One swam out too far

≈ 5 ≈

Other days
it is countries that are distant
Japan   once so close   is far from me
I was almost citizen enough
for the sushi chef to pour me
teriyaki instead of dashi

A person can shift
between such places
They come back   speed off again
like those worlds
at the top of the Faraway Tree
which could have been apple or oak

Some days
worlds of Contentment allow themselves to be summoned
enough for me to taste pickle   or avocado maki

I always said I'd return
Kofu is 20 hours away
That's not far
when you want something badly

This time
I'll be wearing my brightest colours
have you alongside

with all the rain in Japan
a too small umbrella   pale blue
bought in a Tokyo subway

It sits in my bag
a quiet thing
too frail for Cornish storms

but I keep it close   carry it
for when Calm
makes itself absent

I've no softness about myself
on those days
I could float on my back
look towards light & those other unknowable planets

instead of crawling in tangerine cap
pacing the sea   like a swimmer of lanes
in a chemical pool
where Joy is distant

I swim & read in September sun
bring it close   all that's been beyond me
aim to understand what's already close by
waiting to be noticed
brought closer

I pat the dark brown horse
under the oak
Look up through the wiggly leaves
Keep looking up

Purple, Orange

for Tim

Someone mentioned Cold Water Shock
how hearts are frightened in waves. My heart's
never heard of this, shrinks from the very idea.

It reassures me as I swim; my heart accountant-like
with its steady, monotonous work. I've never
told my heart *I love you*. Perhaps now is the time?

I'm dependent. Especially out here.
I stroke on through a heart-breaking morning,
the tide icy grey, my lover alongside. Two hearts

swilling blood, each with their own kink
of personality. A heron pulses overhead,
its heart gearing up for sustained flight

You reach for me and we're kissing, our hearts tremble
out of their dull pump – the heron forgotten –
in the middle of the bay. A place a heart could

(almost) rest, could be itself; our lips like magnets,
we tread water, hearts preparing – like the heron's –
for more. But first the swim back, that distance

to the wall, where two hearts, one purple,
one orange, are daubed against white. I find myself
asking: *Which of our hearts will outlast the other?*

Bardhonek rag Karrek Loos yn Koos

Ty re omgerghynnas gans dowr.
Kastel, penntiow, porth, my a vir orthis
ow tevi sugnogyon, senpeder,
ty yw kemmys moy dhymm
es karrek sevys, Kernewek os ta
mes estren.

Puptra a way a-dro dhis –
astel revadoryon silhouettys, lester-gwari rudh
ow tackya tooth men, kodh dha honan a byffyers splann.

Insta-parys os ta dhyworth an bora, kilva
anvodhek dhe dhemedhyansow gwav,
dewbriesow treylys ha herdhys meusva a-denewen;
processyons a gerdhoryon freth gans aga hi,
tus ow tiskudha nag yns kerensedhek namoy, na fors
pygemmys a wrussons i pe rag chi gans gwel deg.

Ty a dheber pysk, dell dhesevav?
An diswaytyansow munys ma
a dal bos ragwelys.

My a vir orthis – ni oll a vir orthis.
My a omwovynnas a-dro dhe'th poslev, dha yeth,
dismygi hen Frynkek, breselek, managhek.

Hag ena ty a gews orthiv.
My a neuv y'th vogalennow efan,
omlowenhe ynna.

My a lever dhe'm honan nag eus tra vyth yntredhon
marnas ebron ow troyllya,
leverel na'm deur mann
a'th istori, yth yw moy es ragov
dha gara dhyworth pellder. Ottena –
my a'n leveris.

Ty a vor dha skathow ow tesevos
mayth yskinniv, mes an hyns war-tu ha dhis
nyns yw kompes mann. Omblegyans yw.

My a dhege ow dewlagas, ombareusi
rag dha anal vrithel.

Poem for St Michael's Mount

You've surrounded yourself with water.
Castle, cottages, harbour, I watch
you growing succulents, samphire,
you're so much more to me
than a risen rock, you're Cornish
yet other.

Everything moves around you –
paddle boarders in silhouette, a red yacht
tacking at speed, your own pod of bright dolphins.

You're Insta-ready from dawn, reluctant
backdrop to winter weddings,
couples angled and inched to one side;
processions of eager dog walkers,
people finding they're no longer
in love, no matter how much
a house with a view has cost them.

I suppose you eat fish?
These small disappointments
are to be expected.

I look at you – we all look at you.
I consider your accent, your language,
imagine ancient French, military, monastic.

And then you speak to me.
I swim in your elongated vowels,
luxuriate in them.

I tell myself there is nothing between us
but thrashy sky, tell myself I don't care
about your history, that I find it easier
to love you from a distance. There –
I've said it.

You send out your boats, expecting me
to step on; the path to you is far
from straight. It is a submission.

I close my eyes, make myself ready
for your mackerel breath.

October

swimming buoys
removed
the sea unfettered
no rules now

WINTER

Stirred

The ocean
      clear as martini

                washing the pinky-brown flesh
          of my stumbling skeleton self

      I push out into certain numbing

               on into the raw grip
the best narcotic

         What signals the edge
            the turning point
        of a swim?

              Rachel says *Is it knowing how to choose*
        the moment?

I keep on till instinct
        kicks in

       the sense of needing to crawl
    back pounds hot
            as a hangover

I loll for a moment like a woman in a bath
        sniffing at vodka

The town's bells are on me
         tolling nine

          not as far out as I'd thought

I could swim on
      but that's the sea talking

         pulling me
             out with the tide

               of its woozy lotus voice

Cormorant

A bird skims us with its dark whoosh of feathers
Maybe it meant to threaten, to warn us away
from its damp perch on the rock?
The fleet of its wings has me shiver

And what of other times when things were
too close? The man patting the leather seat
of his car, beckoning a schoolgirl over?

Or last month, walking from the village, stepping
out of the whisper of willows, away
from the swampy reeds, I moseyed across
the metal lines of the crossing as the

Cornish Riviera blasted by, missing
the hairs on my arms, by mere centimetres
I shouted at myself, so I could be heard –
though my voice quavered above herons

There's the plane I didn't take, the drink I left
on the bar, the alley I didn't cut through,
the knife my attacker forgot to carry

Looking up out of the steel grey depths
where little light gathers, the cormorant is back
on its rock, neck long, eyes

elsewhere, wings spread wide, as if
there were sun,
as if I'd imagined the whole thing

The Excuses

- ≈ too windy
- ≈ too cold
- ≈ too dangerous/stormy
- ≈ heavy rain
- ≈ low tide
- ≈ foggy
- ≈ just done my hair
- ≈ costume's still wet from earlier/yesterday
- ≈ there's a seal
- ≈ sore throat/can feel one coming on
- ≈ sewage slick
- ≈ jet skiers
- ≈ jellyfish
- ≈ not enough time/too much to do
- ≈ don't want to swim alone
- ≈ afraid, for some other, unspecified reason

Morning, Far West

The sun's muffled, milky, creeping across fields,
coasts. Curlews sense morning as it rolls from
the harbour, puffs of it, heavy-damp. Gulls ruffle
themselves like small dogs. The pearl of light's quiet;
a distant radio searching for the shipping forecast,
dial lost to mizzle. The lamp's too bright for the
hour but gives guidance, lifts a soft corner, slowly,
as if putting an arm out of bed, testing if it really is
morning, allowing the idea in. And beyond, the
headland, a pale thing, half-imagined.

Prayer

as the sun climbs out
                i clamber into
mercury; the sea indifferent, so little
        bothers its armour-smooth surface
except a silver trawler hunting;

my arms launch
              for the horizon
        head bowed
flat palms honouring the moment
        crisp and bright as spurs

Before / After

Artistic discipline and athletic discipline... require the same thing, an unspecial practice: tedious and pitch-black invisible, private as guts, but always sacred.

Leanne Shapton − *Swimming Studies*

My swimming bag − a nylon, striped shopper − hangs on the peg, contains cossie, mat to stand on, shoes for climbing rocks, sunglasses (you never know). I almost forget a towel, it being draped around the house somewhere, in the hope it dries. I wiggle into the navy-blue one-piece, then my ugly-warm joggers, thick (striped) socks, walking boots, a fleece and two jackets, twist my hair into a top-knot, slide hands into mountaineering gloves. I sometimes remember a dark-green woolly hat.

Tim and I walk the same route up Bread Street, down Chapel Street, round the corner, past St Mary's for a blast of what's to come − Westerly? South-Westerly? I'm cheerful, only slightly afraid. It's quiet at 8.45. We cross the road, past the Battery monument, to the rocks, inspect the waves, the swell. And commit. Clothes off as fast as we can, towel on top. We walk rather than run to the sea, concrete bright-cold on our soles.

After, we are louder, half-run to our bags, our skin puckering, clinging to our bones. We stand on our foam mats, show our bodies a towel − mine has a flamingo. I peel off the navy cossie, pull on fleece, joggers, socks, two jackets; always that order, always onto damp, even wet, limbs.

We chat on the way home, walk via the other swimming places − the slipways of the outer harbour, the inner harbour − climb the Abbey Slip granite to the Benbow, swinging our sodden costumes, planning our day − his art, my writing − whether to have beans or avo, and how much toast; who'll have first shower. A ritual, though I'd not seen it that way.

Why?

for Daljit Nagra

You ask why I swim
not how or when or where

I say it takes months to decide
why a person would step out

of a warm bed, hustle into cossie,
joggers, fleeces, socks,

boots, walk eight minutes
to the rocks or harbour and

plunge into December waters
before even a whiff of toast; truth is

I don't know, but this morning
as I swam to the limpet-

laden harbour wall, and back
I was joined by an explosion

of herring gulls, swimming
from the precinct to Poundstretcher

and back, and there and back;
their tough grey alarm-clock voices:

I'm awake; I'm awake; I'm awake
Each bird a sequin stunning the air

How to Be a Cormorant

Forget you haven't eaten
       fish for years
Develop a taste for eels

      Learn to dive
from a position of sitting
            no, squatting
                 on water

Find your mouth
       open, your lips protruding
rigid, hooked, as if wearing a Venetian mask
       your forehead slants
back with fresh emotions

Sense your eyesight's keener
       than ever
especially in the depths

Extend your elegant neck
            expect any size of fish
to swim down it
       swallow whole
salt's provided

Your breath is unmentionable

Keep diving
       it's your obsession

Flap your green-black fingers
       Try harder
Notice how they waft
           Come on, flap as if you truly intend to fly

Find yourself doing so

Give up
        your longing for land
Discover a favourite rock out in the bay
        This is yours
                You may have to share

Learn the tides by your tiny dark heart
Remember, you no longer
        dive through waves
like a would-be surfer
                but skim them
something like a smile
        torturing your beak

You understand cold water
                is essential to your being

Shift your wings
                out from their tight, damp body
peg them to a Westerly
                in the shape of a stylised cross

Stay like this
        with your comrades
until your rock resembles a cemetery
                a near-final scene from *Spartacus*
                        the road to Cavalry

The Source

Dive in / an unadulting / scabbing knees on rocks / Later I'll watch the ooze and settle of its lava // Skin's a leaky boundary / water like a missing father // Do I go further / back to the warm water chamber / where I sloshed for months / knowing nothing / but the tide / of my mum's heartbeat / the rhythm of fluid / whether calm (Mum sleeping) / or bothered (how I like the sea best) / Mum maybe jiving or having sex // Do I go further / before I crawled from the waves / The image I tweeted of an unknown fish / its bright green spine (almost neon) / lover of colour / Ancestor

A History of the Sea

Having mythologised your parentage, we can
only project – let's say a cloud and a grain of salt
Others suggest comets, asteroids, earthquakes
to imply your violence

Who knows when you were born?
Your wrinkles wash up
night after day on this beach

You're essential to my life
to humans, animals, our planet's existence
but what's essential to you?

Does hydrogen make you laugh?
Is it laughter when you explode
into a zawn?

Sailors, pirates, women
with busted mirrors
told your tales in the past
You're tired of being regaled with that giant squid
its skyscraper tentacle
Tell me, was Poseidon a bore?

Jacques Cousteau revealed
what we wish we didn't know –
your relationship with plastic
your pallid reefs
your contretemps with ice caps

You're famous for hosting battles
the effect of your tides on the Armada
We carve the dates of your floods
into granite; we've honoured you this way
But you want more

What's your story?
Why all this emotion?
Do you resent the moon's power?

What became of the sirens?

Whales are your precious things
you've learned their songs

Do you mourn the plesiosaurs?

I chart your affinity
to the four winds
You seem like lovers

We know so little of the future

Cornish dialect word: zawn – fissure in a cliff

The Men

undress, in white stick-on beards
which will mostly come

unstuck; a flotilla of pale maleness
stark against the dark water

the men need to be noticed
their shrieks

echo
across the empty harbour

bodies pinched, in crimson pants
mini Santas, all

Coward

The sea is no colour
I know; brown-grey-green, jostling
twigs, bark, trees

a snaky current
pulling the sky down

My knuckles graze
on a log of oak
lording it in the harbour

I swim through white feathers
Swans elsewhere

Life Underwater

for Hils

The garden willows washed
away, tussocks of marram, jellied
with anemones, the start
of a lively coral

Rosemary – its dull winter
survival – transformed, aromatic, among the salty angel
fish

The bright water
thuds at the see-through back
of the house; expect
sharks, manta rays, perhaps a small whale
Dolphins we're used to

Diving
from the bedroom window, its choice
of springboards, perhaps we'll build
a water slide

The old farm gate
allows everything through as it
rusts in gratitude, made beautiful once more
by whelks, mussels, oysters
offering pearlised over galvanised

Crabs
replace the pond's frogs; bullrushes
and flag iris obliterated for a glisten of kelp
which raves, lissom and lithe, arms
in the air

The oak and sycamore forest
still stands

I give it 30 years

Valentine's Day

What evil joy the storm – George Mackay Brown

I play dead
it's the best I can do

The tide was running
I was alone

I measured each human stroke
each failed swipe at the sea

each semi-coordinated kick
how the railing & steps

– my means of escape –
came no closer

no closer & no closer
With each sweep of arms

my heart thrashed in brine
February the fourteenth –

the sea enthralled
It wanted a body

any body
It had mine

bashed it to & fro
I gulped its foul water

No lifeguard
A domestic behind closed doors

It gloated
at its sodden prize

considered carrying me off
Some part of itself

hesitated
threw me high on the rocks

I landed hip & thigh
scraped against steps

their concrete-barnacle-limpet edge
I scrambled up & up

dragging damp lungs with me
before the sea realised

its mistake
how it had left itself

swimming back out alone

Knowing When to Turn Back

after Elizabeth-Jane Burnett

                  I pound the water
as if attached to a length of elastic
a dark blue mitten
which will never be lost

                  There are no sides to sea swimming
It's like a night at a party, hoping I won't peel open
another gleaming can of Stella

                  like a meal
at my friend's, when I refuse thirds
of salted caramel ice cream, or mid-
way through 10 days' Euro-railing, I realise
I'm not going to reach Istanbul

                  Maybe I'll figure out
I won't touch the sloshy horizon

                  try not to see it
as giving up, but that older sister voice –
instinct – talks loud; her message
in red capitals on each wave

                  I know I need to
reorientate to land

                  Elastic strains against the safety
pin piercing my costume

The Team

Blood dashes to the surface, as if it too wants to plunge through the permeable layer of skin to brine, to wake itself. Heart opens like a young anemone, thudding brighter, brighter, flushing the body tomatoesque. Skin's holding fast, bracing for blood's insistence and the inevitable bash of thigh against rusty railing. Lungs gasp. If other organs grumble at working that bit harder on a Friday morning in February, in rain, I don't hear them above the shrill of upper arms, hanging like pale deflated arm bands, expected to stroke hard in 7° C or less. They do. They hate me for it.

Today the Weather's Too Bad to Swim

The tide has given up
smashing the harbour wall
for now – its twice daily ambush on the town –
knowing it will win, one night, having
catapulted stones through house-high waves
before retreating with its army of horses

swimming out for the thin, bumpy blue line
that meeting of colours
vista of hulking trawlers
Even the sea knows they're a target
too far but the sea likes the excuse
of keeping itself
fit, for tonight's battering at the dark harbour

For now, the sea walks
back from the beach, the sand stunned
The waves know
to the salted minute how long
the dog owners have
to carry their dainty bags of shit before
the sea's outriders rush
right in to sweep them off
their feet and paws

Unknown pools, waist-high
kelp forests, reveal themselves
unused to air or a dog walker's gaze
Mor, mor, mor
The tide looks back
already bored
rumbles from its camp
craves the land so hard
As good a colonizer as any

SPRING

The Bathing Water Quality Inspector

I've left the microscope, desalination kit, my beautiful
chemicals at the lab, where I analyse aqueous data
according to EU Directive 2006/7/EC. There's evidence

of three slurry run-offs this past month. Always the same farm.
The water company holds its nose and releases. Grit
in the surf – a former barn reduced by developers

for yet another holiday home. Here's the lesser contaminants:
dog hair (four varieties); one gannet in an advanced state
of decomposition; shreds of brushed cotton from 1970's pyjamas (men's);

flakes from hardened rubber gloves; six different types
of urine – including my own; mackerel parts (undigested);
Stella, Heineken and the Co-Op's own brand, high-strength cans

(mostly crushed). Oestrogen traces. I'd estimate the percentage of salt
to be 3.5% in late March on a neap tide. Inevitably, there's plastic.
On this stretch it's mostly orange and green nylon nets,

and supposedly biodegradable dog poo bags (with contents),
which I refuse to analyse. Yesterday, I found a love letter, ripped
into bite-sized pieces; biocides; a bull seal's whisker; and surprisingly,

no human sperm, despite Viagra compounds. I also detect
the love of 15 good women and a man's tears. The sunlight
penetration is up to 7mm this morning. But it's boat painting season:

expect particles of arsenic, ammonia, nickel and cadmium.
Faecal matter is to within a percentile point of good bathing water
quality but of course this will change, after heavy rain.

I know you as

mor, mar, mer
call you friend, lover, darling
hating the word

         ocean

I sense you
still don't know my name

I call you
cold thing, brute, destroyer

Your voice's like heavy traffic

        Tell me
what's your safe word?

           You never listen to mine

horizonless day
let this body be elevated
on a cool grey swell

Nothing Biblical

no parting
but some days you sense
makes way
a person's need
of itself
to the States
Atlanticking
the rollers and their moshing
between the mundanity of chores
swimming is the high point of a day
some mornings it allows
the orange buoys pop back up
loll towards Newlyn
even if other things
your list
the sea
a communication
of empathy

of waves
the tide
as if it understands
the sea having plenty
stretching from here
and beyond
there's a pause between
between downpours
you suspect
the sea knows this
ease to a swim
damp Belisha beacons
something to aim for
fall from
you've done this
and you
the sea showing what it can
most days it's enough

A Certain Presence

like someone you should recognise
but fail to

You're tiring on this longer swim
as your partner pushes on towards the rocks

towards the other swimmers
who are pointing

You look back
over your bare left shoulder

as on moorland, when you turn
asking yourself: that glimmer in the fog

 – is that a man?
And it's a stone, or tree, or gorse bush

or nothing, except fear –
putting bodies into landscapes

Again, you turn:
there's a shape to your senses

A knowledge
you're not alone

You step onto the rocks
in tropical print bikini

Wow
That bull seal right behind you

Didn't you see him?
He was massive

Boys and Men

If there's a word for extreme hesitancy, coupled with bravado, I'd like to hear it; it would help describe three boys walking into the sea. One wears a grey T-shirt and blue shorts, as if this could make him more resilient. Turns out, he's the only one to dunk himself; I can't say 'swim', for there's no movement beyond a swift bend in the knees – an instant submersion – no more than a second; he's straight back up with the buoyancy of a mallard. It's good to see him dunk. His two friends wade to the waist; one does no more, the other offers the length of his hair to the water, throws his head back – extravagant – like an actor in a shampoo ad.

The week before; three men, wearing those extra-long swimming 'shorts' – the sort you'd choose if you didn't fancy yourself with browner legs – are shouting at each other *Get In*. They whoop and swear at the sea – at the cold – possibly at their exhilaration (but I suspect I'm projecting). Or maybe their noise is aimed at passers-by on the prom. *LOOK AT US*, as if we hadn't already swum that day but had drawn slightly less attention to ourselves.

There are different ways to go loud. I return to the lad in the grey T-shirt – the slightly chubby one. He was quieter than the rest, didn't splash his mates, just gave his body what it needed – a cooling, no more – and strode out; T-shirt puckering at his chest, at the round of his tummy. He walked to his towel with a dignity I might learn from.

Mordrik

Skerries rise
unbidden

What little water remains
is unsure

whether to show off
or apologize

Barnacles
sunbathe in their billions

Starfish strand
before

dangling
from a gull's beak

a late breakfast
of legs

Kelp
dries itself

Blennies
sink as best they can

A fox
bounces across the beach

leaps from island to island
russet

against black rock
fossicking for shag's eggs

Listen
no vixen bark

just the murmur
of a boat's engine

and the shush
of a would-be wave

Kernewek (Cornish) word: mordrik – low tide

In a Rock Pool, with Borrowed Cossie

for Jude

Your friends have already swum, are sat, smug
with sarnies and flasks. Even the dog's been in.
You sit, fully clothed, feeling like someone's mother.
Jude says: *Why not swim in my cossie?*
Hands you a damp, black one-piece, with fancy straps.
Use my towel too, it's not that wet. You strip
with your back to your friends, the fisherman, the dog,
pull the moist cling of nylon up; it twangs into place.

Your splash is delicious; sea greens tickle, the surface
shifts, makes room. You swim three strokes to the pool's
granite limit, where rollers will thunder through
in under an hour, restoring this spot to its full invisibility.
You float, still, in the hope blennies will arrive.
Only the dog stirs, shivers; the fisherman curses the tide.

And if there were no sea?

no shushing of the pull / no shimmer of summer / no knowledge of splash / no repetition of clouds / no clouds / no splendour of kelp / no fish / no study of scales / no silhouette of oystercatcher / the moon on repeat / no islands / no need for ships / storms would laze in their beds / no Speedos / no coastal erosion / all of us living inland / no salt / no shells / no need to row / no *Jaws* / no glamour of rock pools / nowhere for the sun to swim / no rivers / rain unknown / no place to drown

The Sound of Swimming's Like a Hand Swishing in a Grey Bucket

Oh

A bright inbreath as a swimmer drops
disturbing the glitterball frenzy of sun on sea

A tanker twists on its anchor
to the silent disco, showing its port
its starboard

Bleddy lovely today, isn't it? So calm

You hear the tide
– its accent – only in stillness
The rest is noise

A loud trail of Body
Shop White Musk sings out
as a Great Western train surfs the coast

a quiet reflection
in the bay, a sleek sea serpent
its slow motion hiss

My Friend's Bath

after Amy Lowell

Cutting brambles on my friend's land, I've yanked briars thick as my middle finger from the lower reaches of willow and rosemary; their yellows, their soft blues, come to reflect in a white room, come creeping through slats with late afternoon light.

I pull off jeans and sweatshirt, socks with thorns in their pill. The bulbous bath, with its animal feet, squats in the clearing of the room. Water arrives, somehow.

My gently ripped hands swish their sting, plunging again in the heat of thickets. I step in, stepping off the land. No room to swim. I sink my shoulders, propping ankles on the bath's lip.

Baths disappoint. The water cools, bubbles fail, the scent rarely fulfils. My water – I feel I've owned it – inches down the enamel. But it's done a job. My neck supports my head, heavy as a bullish bluebell, while this spine uncurls in the haze of late afternoon, like a fine, April, fern.

SUMMER

Dive

Have you seen a body
after water? I've seen a dolphin
innards bright pink
through lacerations

So many men on the trawlers
never learn to swim – better to die easy
than prolong it

This, our first, our only
dive – no time to think of lungs
bursting, our shocking selves
hanging
in suspension

flesh like the chewed remains
of a dog's toy
unidentifiable blobs of matter

We're fully sunk now, irretrievable
I sensed we wouldn't be ones to rise
and float
having no thoughts
of heaven

Last thing I saw –
the woodgrain of the wreck's hull
marred by the crust of animals
their dull sparkle
their almost diamanté

One Flesh

flap of skin between thumb
and index finger

this web
this water trapper

like a swan or mallard's foot

Crawl School

I said yes to snorkelling in Malindi
all those blue and yellow fish   looming
I lashed out   gave panic its buoyancy
                wanted nothing but the boat

I'm still trying to get over that afternoon

≈ 2 ≈

Kelp knows my fear
the way a collie senses weakness
in one who's scared   but will persevere

≈ 3 ≈

I practise in the bathroom sink
place my nose
            mouth
                eyes
in four inches of water
study the plug
it needs scrubbing

breathe out slowly

        But the sea's something else

≈ 4 ≈

How glad I am of this morning's fog
borrowed goggles misting
weed   rocks   fish

I thrust my face into the flowing world
forsaking the known

I only see the bull seal
as I pat my face dry

≈ 5 ≈

Burping on every other breath
face in the sea   air as fear
Ella says   *Breathe out*
through your nose   bring in
crawl arms   breathe out
for four   then five

Again   I open my eyes
underwater

breath bubbling in my ears
waves   the long grey of panic

everything tight   in my mind
my skin
                    my head shouts
to itself

of a knowledge
          I've never been taught

≈ 6 ≈

Plunge my face back in
gulp and cough out the sea

A long spaghetti of weed drifts
silver fish pulse

It's all too brief

                but I'm there

the slightest of breaths
pearls from my nose
Curl your arms over

I swim like a wonky windmill
come up   snotty   gasping for air
fearing my newfound power

≈ 7 ≈

take sips of air
        under your armpit
while pulling the sea
        through your paddle-hands
arm brushing your thigh
        no splash
go slowly
        try to trickle the breath
out from your nostrils
        don't hold your breath

≈ 8 ≈

I live for that snatch of air
to the left   to the right
                        above the waves'
race   holding my breath
or blurt out Jacques Cousteau-
size bubbles from my mouth
not my nose

I roll   a lumbering thing
unsure of my strength
the newness of this stroke

the head-down rolling
is also new   to this body
after 57 years of movement
I'm nothing

like a baby   everything like a baby
proud in this strange self
of propulsion   face down
arms curling   legs kicking

#nightswim

instead of noticing the water's texture   i'm struck by how the sea
greets the night   its notoriety   above a whiff of diesel   the arcade's
trancey lights shiver across the bay   everyday herring gulls transform
into a metallica of sound & silver   me & nat push out   tim & jason
splash behind   a shifting square in the ocean   on the easy swim to
the first buoy   i'd hoped for quiet   our shouts echo   the buoy busy
dissolving into dusk   i kick its tether of weed & slime   a scream
hangs above me   so *this* is night swimming   my friends' laughter
hurries in   on the backwash   dry as a star   the scream carries itself
as fear   a gansey's midnight blue   wraps around my cossie   i look
to penzance   red   green   yellow   white   pulse from the prom
colours tread water   dazzle   before sinking   in formation   we
slow backstroke   to the black rocks   wanting the swim to last
cooling   i haul myself out   human again   grasp the antler felt on the
rusty railing   its gorgeous sea moss of welcome   to land   torches
calling to clothes   dress fast   a cork high dives   we drink fizz as
if toasting the froth of waves   as if toasting ourselves   the bubbles
speak   of surfing & sharks   the fins become taller & taller   later i
dream of the whales of instagram   swimming towards our town

Watched by a Pale Hermit Crab

As if it feels the need to produce something
on a Monday morning, the sea tenders
a lazy swell, before giving in to the heat.
We crunch dark wrack into the semi-cold,
water like green vodka, before swimming out.
I float, an ungainly star, ears attune
underwater to the shush-bubble of a wave
but I'm interrupted – Tim making *Jaws* music
– *dood-dood, dood-dood, dood-dood, dood-dood,*
dood-ah-da, his fin of quiff up close; he lands
a kiss on my cheek. We swim parallel to the beach
to our jumble of possessions: our bikes
like cut-outs against the dunes. We wade
back over pebbles, altered animals

On Not Getting In

We walked six good miles
across the moor
heaved ourselves down
to the black lichened rocks

I hoped to leave
my cossie in the airless rucksack
There was no one to see

Wanted to show off
my strength and bravado
to say I'd swum from those rocks

But my guts turned to water
as the sea grabbed for my shins
crashed at the base of the cliff

For once, I listened to my body

I know the tide
throws its voice, I've learnt Sea
There's no word for No

only for climbing back up
on all fours, a river running
the length of a spine

Golden Shovel: After a Lillicrap Chilcott Ad

Even out here, there's no overlooking
the impact of second homes of Mousehole, Marazion, how tranquil
they are in winter. Cobbled streets talk to themselves. Waters
appear shallow; they're deeper than you think. And
I swim away from the stony strip of beach
If only everyone who grew up here, people of
Cornwall, could find a home. Squalling Saint
Ives – Porth Ia – avoided by locals. Who truly lives in St Ives?
Others' yachts yawn in the harbour
Downalong, Upalong, every house a holiday let. And
I keep swimming the bay
but this send-up of Kernow as somewhere ideal
carries on, while Cornish key workers are forced up-country; as
so many love Cornwall, at least for a
weekend. Fields churned up for more holiday
homes; the finest crop. Who else can afford the rental?
Estate agents deeming a flat or a house a 'property'
adds thousands to the asking price, with or
without a sea glimpse. Families turned out as
Airbnb kills the place it says it adores. A
school closes, a grocer's shuts. There's a private
school in Truro; Waitrose online. Who invented the word 'bolthole'?
What are we buying into? Offers
on a postcard, please. Look around
a one-bed house in St Ives, yours for £600,000.

Kernewek (Cornish) words: Porth Ia – St Ives; Kernow – Cornwall

The Barbs

As the sun glees
on dark water
                a jellyfish tells its joke
The first sting
after thousands of swims
from the Battery

I tread water
study how the thin skin
of my wrist has raised itself
puckering pink
in mild indignation
                      Probably a compass
Chrysaora hysoscella
I saw nothing
but felt the cool, brown
bumping body

A few days back, another such
sensation, much more
unexpected – the writer –
the big fish
who went for me
                  raised up welts
of class and gender
those infested barbs
I was stunned –
prey all over again

A reminder of the male poets
who talked
only to each other
on the festival panel
                  I had to thump
the table to be heard
They strolled
to the pub, without me

The venom coursed for days
worse at night, contracted
around my heart, brain,
nervous system
                    My cnidocytes
unprepared
but the men knew
where to attack

A jellyfish is just doing its job
its sting arbitrary
non-judgmental
                    I'd always feared
the nematocysts' bite, but the pain
was momentary

From that lacy moment on, I was free
to go out of my depth, having passed
an initiation
                    This morning, I swam
to the fifth buoy and back
the furthest I've dared

Counting each buoy
the pain lessened
I've been raised to be
stronger than this
                    On the return
I cursed those writers
and their male tentacles
with every stroke of that salted mile
where I was in my element

Cornwall: Sea Safety & Swim Tips

Always swim

failing this

make your face cold

Protect your

reaction to the cold water

Suggestions

from a pharmacy

are very popular

and

come

highly recommended

Bring a

good idea   get all the layers on

Nearly all swimmers feel fantastic

This is called continued cooling

often mistaken for the term   cold water

After your swim   forget

sustained energy

Tip:

Ensure you have not over tightened your   strap

and

pop out

when you plan to go for a swim,
imagine

The empty   tide
fills   .
the
body   This may be
when it's
ebbing
In the sixth hour
you can see
swimming has a big impact
we are going
in the other
direction   for

if you become   cold, the return journey is
much easier
use the

high
for 20 mins
swimming in the
moon

adds to the strength

Mount   the tide is   A useful phrase

Finally

in the kelp forest

the first time she finds herself   among brown strands
between fear and wonder   floating   in this other world
of upside down   a place a person could wed herself to   so
much dank silence   beyond her breath   the gentle murmur
of limbs   in suspension   their arc and splay   there's no
peace like this in the dry country   she's like a body in a jar
at the lab   but keeps her Dutch colours   sliding her mind
through slender lengths of weed   fabric-like   plastic-like
part translucent   part shine   like nothing else but kelp   her
restless hair goes on its own pulsing journey   she forgets   for
blissed moments   she can't breathe here   this isn't air
waves nudge overhead   it's like any place almost visited   say
a city   say Seville   and she talks half-seriously   half what-if
of how she might live here   the kelp wafts in welcome   displays
its tentacles   as she refuses neoprene   longs for kelp's beckon
and touch   longs to pass as a local   a strange fish for sure   but
one who could belong

Acknowledgements

'in the kelp forest' won the 2021 Keats-Shelley Prize for Poetry, and a selection of poems from *Battery Rocks* was shortlisted for the 2021 Alpine Prize.

Some of these poems were previously published in: *Bad Lilies, Berlin Lit; Finished Creatures; The Keats-Shelley Review; Magma; Poetry Ireland Review; Poetry Wales; Spelt; 10 Poems on Swimming,* edited by Samantha Wynne-Rhydderch (Candlestick Press, 2022); *10 Poems from Cornwall,* edited by Katrina Naomi (Candlestick Press, 2023); *Festival in a Book,* edited by Liz Lefroy (904 Press, 2023), and *Same But Different,* by Helen Mort & Katrina Naomi (Hazel Press, 2021).

My deepest thanks to the Society of Authors for an Authors' Foundation Award and the Arthur Welton Award for this collection, and to the Royal Literary Fund for financial support, and to Cultivator Cornwall for a Creative Investment Award. Thanks too to Brisons Veor, Gladstone's Library, Hils Tranter and Morrab Library for space to write.

Thank you to Fiona Benson, Kim Moore, Daljit Nagra, Roger Robinson and Penelope Shuttle, and to all members of The Group for advice and support. With love to everyone who swims off the Battery Rocks and to swimming coach extraordinaire, Ella Turk-Richards, for helping me to put my face in the water. Thanks to Marcus Stanton.

Diolch to my editors at Seren, Zoë Brigley and Rhian Edwards, and to all the staff, including design, promotion, sales, finance and administration.

Meur ras bras to Steve Penhaligon for helping me revise my Kernewek translation of 'Poem for St Michael's Mount'.

Thanks to my friends and my sister for all their support and kindness.

And finally, thank you to Tim Ridley for swims, hot chocolate and love.

About Katrina Naomi

Katrina Naomi has won the Arthur Welton Award for her fourth full collection, *Battery Rocks* (Seren, 2024). The collection contains the poem 'in the kelp forest', which won the prestigious Keats-Shelley Prize for Poetry. Katrina received an Authors' Foundation Award from the Society of Authors for work on her third collection, *Wild Persistence* (Seren, 2020). She has a PhD in Creative Writing from Goldsmiths College. Katrina's work has been broadcast on Radio 4's *Front Row, Poetry Please*, BBC TV *Spotlight* and on Poems on the Underground. Her second poetry collection, *The Way the Crocodile Taught Me*, (Seren, 2016), was chosen by Foyles Bookshop as one of its Foyles' Five for Poetry. She was the first writer-in-residence at the Brontë Parsonage Museum in Haworth, W Yorks. Her recent pamphlets include *Typhoon Etiquette*, (Verve Poetry Press) published following an Arts Council-funded trip to Japan, *Same But Different* with Helen Mort (Hazel Press), which won a Saboteur Award, and *An Alfoxden Journal* with Sara Hudston (Hazel Press). She was highly commended in the 2017 Forward Prize for Poetry.

Katrina has been poet in residence at the Arnolfini, and at Gladstone's Library in North Wales where she wrote a sequence on the Suffragettes, published by Rack Press as *Hooligans*. Her debut collection *The Girl with the Cactus Handshake* received an Arts Council Award and was shortlisted for the London New Poetry Award. Her pamphlet *Lunch at the Elephant & Castle* won the 2008 Templar Poetry Pamphlet Competition and her pamphlet *Charlotte Brontë's Corset* was published to acclaim by the Brontë Society. She is a Hawthornden Fellow, a tutor for Arvon and Ty Newydd, and runs Poetry Surgeries for the Poetry Society. She is published by *The TLS, The Poetry Review* and *Poetry Wales*. She received an award from the Royal Literary Fund in 2014 for her writing. She enjoys performing her poetry and collaborating with visual artists, musicians and film-makers. She is originally from Margate and lives in Cornwall.

www.katrinanaomi.co.uk

@katrinanaomipoet – Instagram

@KatrinaNaomi – Twitter/X